Also by Donald Revell

Collections of Poetry

The Bitter Withy, Alice James Books, 2009
A Thief of Strings, Alice James Books, 2007
Pennyweight Windows: New & Selected Poems,
Alice James Books, 2005
My Mojave, Alice James Books, 2003
Arcady, Wesleyan University Press, 2002
There Are Three, Wesleyan University Press, 1998
Beautiful Shirt, Wesleyan University Press, 1994
Erasures, Wesleyan University Press, 1992
New Dark Ages, Wesleyan University Press, 1990
The Gaza of Winter, University of Georgia Press, 1988
From the Abandoned Cities, Harper & Row, 1983

Prose

The Art of Attention: A Poet's Eye, Graywolf Press, 2007
Invisible Green: Selected Prose, Omnidawn Publishing, 2005

Translations

The Illuminations, by Arthur Rimbaud, Omnidawn Publishing, 2009
A Season in Hell, by Arthur Rimbaud, Omnidawn Publishing, 2007
*The Self-Dismembered Man: Selected Later Poems of
Guillaume Apollinaire*, Wesleyan University Press, 2004
Alcools: Poems of Guillaume Apollinaire, Wesleyan University Press, 1995

Last Verses

Last Verses

by

Jules Laforgue

Translated by

Donald Revell

OMNIDAWN PUBLISHING
RICHMOND, CALIFORNIA
2011

Cover Art by Odilon Redon, *Five Butterflies*, 1912
Watercolor on wove paper, 270 mm x 211 mm (10.2 x 8.3 inches)
Collection of Mr. and Mrs. Paul Mellon
Image courtesy of the Board of Trustees,
National Gallery of Art, Washington D. C.

Book cover and interior design by Ken Keegan

Offset printed in the United States on archival, acid-free recycled paper
by Thomson-Shore, Inc., Dexter, Michigan

Omnidawn Publishing is committed to preserving ancient
forests and natural resources. We elected to print this title on
30% postconsumer recycled paper, processed chlorine-free. As
a result, for this printing, we have saved:

3 Trees (40' tall and 6-8" diameter)
1,361 Gallons of Wastewater
1 million BTUs of Total Energy
86 Pounds of Solid Waste
302 Pounds of Greenhouse Gases

Omnidawn Publishing made this paper choice because our
printer, Thomson-Shore, Inc., is a member of Green Press
Initiative, a nonprofit program dedicated to supporting authors,
publishers, and suppliers in their efforts to reduce their use of
fiber obtained from endangered forests.

For more information, visit www.greenpressinitiative.org

Environmental impact estimates were made using the Environmental Defense
Paper Calculator. For more information visit: www.edf.org/papercalculator

Library of Congress Catalog-in-Publication Data
Laforgue, Jules, 1860-1887.
 [Derniers vers. English & French]
Last verses / by Jules Laforgue ; translated by Donald Revell.
 p. cm.
Poems.
English and French text on facing pages.
ISBN 978-1-890650-54-4 (pbk. : alk. paper)
1. Laforgue, Jules, 1860-1887--Translations into English.
 I. Revell, Donald, 1954- II. Title.
PQ2323.L8D4713 2011
841'.8--dc23

2011026868

Published by Omnidawn Publishing, Richmond, California
www.omnidawn.com   (510) 237-5472   (800) 792-4957
10 9 8 7 6 5 4 3 2 1
ISBN: 978-1-890650-54-4

Acknowledgments

"Simply Agony" first appeared in the July 2011 issue of Eleven Eleven, whose editors we thank for their support.

These translations are dedicated to
Jeffrey Warshaw

Table of Contents

A Note on the Translation

Derniers Vers was first published in 1890, three years after the poet's death. Nevertheless, eleven of the twelve poems (i.e., all of them, save the final piece) appeared in magazines during his lifetime. Critics argue as to whether these dozen constitute a single poem, a poetic sequence, or simply an unfinished collection. *Qui sait?* But all agree that *Derniers Vers* is the first true volume of free verse in the French language. Laforgue was an ardent reader of Whitman, after all, and he even published several translations from *Leaves of Grass* in the magazine *La Vogue*.

Still, we must not think of *his* free verse in any American sense of that elusive term. The poems of *Derniers Vers* rely fervently and beautifully upon rhyme and upon tightly wrought individual stanzas. Their freedom is in the cadences, in the variety of line lengths (wild departures from the standard alexandrine), and in their collaging of poetic, bathetic, and tragic idioms. Trying to bring a sense of Laforgue's innovations across into our American English, I have chosen to rely upon alliteration, repetition, internal rhyme and, from time to time, the argot of popular culture, hoping to preserve as much of his music as possible without ever downplaying his boldness, his hilarity, his heartbreak and his purist's savagery.

DERNIERS VERS

Jules Laforgue

LAST VERSES

Translated by
Donald Revell

I have not the art to reckon my groans [...]
Thine evermore, Most dear lady, whilst this machine is to him.
                                         J.L.

OPHELIA: He took me by the wrist, and held me hard;
    Then goes he to the length of all his arm,
    And, with his other hand thus o'er his brow,
    He falls to such perusal of my face,
    As he would draw it. Long stay'd he so:
    At last,—a little shaking of mine arm,
    And thrice his head thus waving up and down,
    He rais'd a sigh so piteous and profound,
    That it did seem to shatter all his bulk,
    And end his being. That done he lets me go,
    And with his head over his shoulder turn'd
    He seem'd to find his way without his eyes;
    For out o' doors he went without their help,
    And to the last bended their light on me.

POLONIUS: This is the very ecstasy of love.

I have not the art to reckon my groans [...]
Thine evermore, Most dear lady, whilst this machine is to him.
                                                            J.L.

OPHELIA: He took me by the wrist, and held me hard;
    Then goes he to the length of all his arm,
    And, with his other hand thus o'er his brow,
    He falls to such perusal of my face,
    As he would draw it. Long stay'd he so:
    At last,—a little shaking of mine arm,
    And thrice his head thus waving up and down,
    He rais'd a sigh so piteous and profound,
    That it did seem to shatter all his bulk,
    And end his being. That done he lets me go,
    And with his head over his shoulder turn'd
    He seem'd to find his way without his eyes;
    For out o' doors he went without their help,
    And to the last bended their light on me.

POLONIUS: This is the very ecstasy of love.

I. L'hiver qui vient

Blocus sentimental! Messageries du Levant!...
Oh! tombée de la pluie! Oh! tombée de la nuit,
Oh! le vent!...
La Toussaint, la Noël, et la Nouvelle Année,
Oh, dans les bruines, toutes mes cheminées!...
D'usines...

On ne peut plus s'asseoir, tous les bancs sont mouillés;
Crois-moi, c'est bien fini jusqu'à l'année prochaine,
Tous les bancs sont mouillés, tant les bois sont rouillés,
Et tant les cors ont fait ton ton, ont fait ton taine!...

Ah, nuées accourues des côtes de la Manche,
Vous nous avez gâté notre dernier dimanche.

Il bruine;
Dans la forêt mouillée, les toiles d'araignées
Ploient sous les gouttes d'eau, et c'est leur ruine.
Soleils plénipotentiaires des travaux en blonds Pactoles
Des spectacles agricoles,
Où êtes-vous ensevelis?
Ce soir un soleil fichu gît au haut du coteau
Gît sur le flanc, dans les genêts, sur son manteau,
Un soleil blanc comme un crachat d'estaminet
Sur une litière de jaunes genêts
De jaunes genêts d'automne.
Et les cors lui sonnent!
Qu'il revienne....
Qu'il revienne à lui!
Taïaut! Taïaut! et hallali!
O triste antienne, as-tu fini!...
Et font les fous!...
Et il gît là, comme une glande arrachée dans un cou,
Et il frissonne, sans personne!...

I. The Winter Ahead

Sentimental blockade! Frozen Middle Eastern parcel service!...
How the rain falls! How the night falls,
How the wind!...
All Saints', Christmas, New Year's Day,
How in drizzling rain, all my chimney-stones!...
I mean smokestacks...

Nowhere to sit, all the benches are wet;
Believe me, it's a washout until next year,
All the benches are wet, even the trees have rusted,
And the horns have sounded tantivy, have sounded tan-ti-vy!...

Rushing down from the Channel coast, thick clouds
Spoiled our last weekend.

It's drizzling;
In the sodden forest, spiderwebs
Bend under plops of raindrops, and that's the end of them.
Where are you buried
Plenipotentiary suns of agricultural labor fairs
Blond as the river where Midas washed himself?
Tonight the dying sun sprawls on a hilltop,
Turns onto his side, in the heather, in his overcoat.
A sun as white as barfly's phlegm
On a litter of yellow heather,
Yellow autumn heather.
And the hunting horns call to him!
Awake!
Up and awake!
Tally-ho! Tally-ho! View halloo!
Oh sad refrain, you're finished!
And in a fool's game!...
He just lies there, like a gland torn out of somebody's throat,
Shivering, utterly alone.

Allons, allons, et hallali!
C'est l'Hiver bien connu qui s'amène;
Oh! les tournants des grandes routes,
Et sans petit Chaperon Rouge qui chemine!…
Oh! leurs ornières des chars de l'autre mois,
Montant en don quichottesques rails
Vers les patrouilles des nuées en déroute
Que le vent malmène vers les transatlantiques bercails!…
Accélérons, accélérons, c'est la saison bien connue, cette fois.
Et le vent, cette nuit, il en a fait de belles!
O dégâts, ô nids, ô modestes jardinets!
Mon cœur et mon sommeil: ô échos des cognées!…

Tous ces rameaux avaient encor leurs feuilles vertes,
Les sous-bois ne sont plus qu'un fumier de feuilles mortes;
Feuilles, folioles, qu'un bon vent vous emporte
Vers les étangs par ribambelles,
Ou pour le feu du garde-chasse,
Ou les sommiers des ambulances
Pour les soldats loin de la France.

C'est la saison, c'est la saison, la rouille envahit les masses,
La rouille ronge en leurs spleens kilométriques
Les fils télégraphiques des grandes routes où nul ne passe.

Les cors, les cors, les cors—mélancoliques!…
Mélancoliques!…
S'en vont, changeant de ton,
Changeant de ton et de musique,
Ton ton, ton taine, ton ton!…
Les cors, les cors, les cors!…
S'en sont allés au vent du Nord.

Je ne puis quitter ce ton: que d'échos!…
C'est la saison, c'est la saison, adieu vendanges!…
Voici venir les pluies d'une patience d'ange,
Adieu vendanges, et adieu tous les paniers,
Tous les paniers Watteau des bourrées sous les marronniers,

Let's go, let's go, tally-ho!
Old Man Winter's on his way;
Oh! the treacherous bends in the highway,
And Little Red Riding Hood's gone for the day!...
Oh! the October wheel-ruts
Climbing Don Quixote train tracks
Into flocks of bleating clouds
Harried by the wind into oceanic sheepfolds!
Move along, move along, you know what winter's like.
Last night the winds wreaked havoc!
Oh damages, oh bird's nests, oh humble kitchen gardens!
My heart, my sleep: oh echoes of axes!

Only yesterday, all these branches were green,
But today the underwood is a manure of dead leaves;
Leaves, little leaves, may a kind wind carry you
In droves to the ponds,
Into the gamekeeper's fire,
Into ambulance mattresses
Meant for soldiers far from home.

'Tis the season, 'tis the season; rust invades the scrap-heaps,
Rust eats at the metric boredom
Of telegraph wires strung along abandoned roads.

The horns, the horns, the horns—melancholy!...
Melancholy!...
They depart, changing tone,
Changing tone and tune,
Tantivy, tantivy, tan-ti-vy!...
The horns, the horns, the horns!...
Gone far away on the North wind.

The tune got stuck in my head; so many echoes!...
'Tis the season, 'tis the season, goodbye vineyards!
Behold the angelic, patient rains,
Goodbye vineyards, goodbye wicker baskets
And Watteau petticoats tossed under chestnut trees.

C'est la toux dans les dortoirs du lycée qui rentre,
C'est la tisane sans le foyer,
La phtisie pulmonaire attristant le quartier,
Et toute la misère des grands centres.

Mais, lainages, caoutchoucs, pharmacie, rêve,
Rideaux écartés du haut des balcons des grèves
Devant l'océan de toitures des faubourgs,
Lampes, estampes, thé, petits-fours,
Serez-vous pas mes seules amours!…
(Oh! et puis, est-ce que tu connais, outre les pianos,
Le sobre et vespéral mystère hebdomadaire
Des statistiques sanitaires
Dans les journaux?)

Non, non! C'est la saison et la planète falote!
Que l'autan, que l'autan
Effiloche les savates que le Temps se tricote!
C'est la saison, oh déchirements! c'est la saison!
Tous les ans, tous les ans,
J'essaierai en chœur d'en donner la note.

There's coughing in the dormitories of a new semester,
Snack time in the drafty classrooms,
Tuberculosis glooming the neighborhoods,
Cosmopolitan misery.

But woolens, galoshes, drug stores, dreams,
Curtains parted on riverside balconies
Facing oceans of roof tiles,
Lamps, engravings, tea, finger cakes,
Won't you be my only loves!…
(Oh, by the way, have you seen, atop pianos,
The sober evening weekly mystery
Of the health statistics
In newspapers?)

No! T'is the season, and this is still our colorless Earth!
How the southerly wind, how the southerly wind
Unravels the bed-slippers Time's been knitting!
'Tis the season! Oh heartbreak! 'Tis the season!
Every year, each and every year,
I croon the tune.

II. Le mystère des trois cors

Un cor dans la plaine
Souffle à perdre haleine,
Un autre, du fond des bois,
Lui répond;
L'un chante ton taine
Aux forêts prochaines,
Et l'autre ton ton
Aux échos des monts.

Celui de la plaine
Sent gonfler ses veines,
Ses veines du front;
Celui du bocage,
En vérité, ménage
Ses jolis poumons.

—Où donc tu te caches,
Mon beau cor de chasse?
Que tu es méchant!

—Je cherche ma belle,
Là-bas, qui m'appelle
Pour voir le Soleil couchant.

—Taïaut! Taïaut! Je t'aime!
Hallali! Roncevaux!

—Être aimé est bien doux;
Mais, le Soleil qui se meurt, avant tout!

Le Soleil dépose sa pontificale étole,
Lâche les écluses du Grand-Collecteur
En mille Pactoles
Que les plus artistes
De nos liquoristes

II. The Mystery of Three Horns

Out on the plain a horn
Blows insanely
While deep in the woods
Another replies;
The first sings yoo-hoo
To neighboring treetops,
And the second, whoo-hoo
To the echoing hills.

The one on the plain
Is blowing its brains out,
Blue veins bulge on its brow;
But tell the truth and shame the Devil,
The one in the woods
Is very careful of its pretty lungs.

—Where are you hiding
Handsome horn of the huntsmen?
How naughty you are!

—I seek my darling
Over there, she's calling,
She wants me to watch the sun go down.

—Tally-ho! How I love you!
Tally-ho! Roncevaux!

—It's nice to be loved;
But the dying sun comes first!

The Sun undresses, casting off its papal garments,
Opens the sewers
Into a thousand mythic rivers
Unscrupulous bootleggers
Poison with fiery

Attisent de cent fioles de vitriol oriental!…
Le sanglant étang, aussitôt s'étend, aussitôt s'étale,
Noyant les cavales du quadrige
Qui se cabre, et qui patauge, et puis se fige
Dans ces déluges de bengale et d'alcool!…

Mais les durs sables et les cendres de l'horizon
Ont vite bu tout cet étalage des poisons.

Ton ton ton taine, les gloires!….

Et les cors consternés
Se retrouvent nez à nez;

Ils sont trois;
Le vent se lève, il commence à faire froid.

Ton ton ton taine, les gloires!…

«—Bras-dessus, bras-dessous,
«Avant de rentrer chacun chez nous,
«Si nous allions boire
«Un coup?»

Pauvres cors! pauvres cors!
Comme ils dirent cela avec un rire amer!
(Je les entends encor).

Le lendemain, l'hôtesse du *Grand-Saint-Hubert*
Les trouva tous trois morts.

On fut quérir les autorités
De la localité,

Qui dressèrent procès-verbal
De ce mystère très immoral.

Phials of Asian vitriol!...
Bloody sewage floods the town, it's in all the papers,
It drowned some horses,
They reared and floundered and froze
In a deluge of Chinese New Year fireworks and booze!...

But the cruel sand and cinders of sundown
Swallowed all the poison.

Tantivy, tan-ti-vy, the glory!...

Much to their dismay
The horns stand face to face;

They are three;
The wind's picking up, it's getting cold.

Tantivy, tan-ti-vy, the glory!

"Arm in arm,
Let's each of us, and why not,
Grab a drink
Before we go home?"

Poor old horns!
So much bitterness, even in their laughter!
(I can still hear them laughing.)

Next day, the barmaid from the *Grand Saint-Hubert*
Found the three of them stone dead.

The cops and the coroner
Were called in,

And in due course they wrote a report
Of this most depraved of mysteries.

III. Dimanches

Bref, j'allais me donner d'un «Je vous aime»
Quand je m'avisai non sans peine
Que d'abord je ne me possédais pas bien moi-même.

(Mon Moi, c'est Galathée aveuglant Pygmalion!
Impossible de modifier cette situation.)

Ainsi donc, pauvre, pâle et piètre individu
Qui ne croit à son Moi qu'à ses moments perdus,
Je vis s'effacer ma fiancée
Emportée par le cours des choses.
Telle l'épine voit s'effeuiller,
Sous prétexte de soir sa meilleure rose.

Or, cette nuit anniversaire, toutes les Walkyries du vent
Sont revenues beugler par les fentes de ma porte:
Væ soli!
Mais, ah! qu'importe?
Il fallait m'en étourdir avant!
Trop tard! ma petite folie est morte!
Qu'importe *Væ soli!*
Je ne retrouverai plus ma petite folie.

Le grand vent bâillonné,
S'endimanche enfin le ciel du matin.
Et alors, eh! allez donc, carillonnez,
Toutes cloches des bons dimanches!
Et passez layettes et collerettes et robes blanches
Dans un frou-frou de lavande et de thym
Vers l'encens et les brioches!
Tout pour la famille, quoi! *Væ soli!* C'est certain.

La jeune demoiselle à l'ivoirin paroissien
Modestement rentre au logis.
On le voit, son petit corps bien reblanchi

III. Sundays

To make a long story short, I'd nearly
Given myself away, saying "I love you."
Then I realized that I was crazy.

(My *Self*? It's Galatea blinding Pygmalion!
Impossible to modify *that* situation.)

And so, poor, pale, pitiful man,
Believing in my Self almost never,
I saw my true love disappear,
Borne away by the way things go.
I was a thorn in the dark,
And she was a wind-blown rose.

On this anniversary night, all the wind-blown Valkyries
Come back bellowing through cracks in the door:
Only the lonely!
So what?
I should have been drunk from the start!
It's too late now! Baby-doll's dead!
Only the lonely, big deal!
Baby-doll's dead and gone.

The wind's been muzzled,
The morning sky's been dressed for church.
All right then, bells, ring out,
All you Sunday bells, ring out!
Put on your baby clothes and snowy robes,
Wiggle your lavender frou-frou
Into the incense clouds and buttered rolls!
Family first! *Only the lonely!* So it goes.

The girl with the ivory prayer book
Hurries, head down, home.
Just look at her, whiter than white,

29

Sait qu'il appartient
A un tout autre passé que le mien!

Mon corps, ô ma sœur, a bien mal à sa belle âme...

Oh! voilà que ton piano
Me recommence, si natal maintenant!
Et ton cœur qui s'ignore s'y ânonne
En ritournelles de bastringues à tout venant,
Et ta pauvre chair s'y fait mal!...
A moi, Walkyries!
Walkyries des hypocondries et des tueries!

Ah! que je te les tordrais avec plaisir,
Ce corps bijou, ce cœur à ténor,
Et te dirais leur fait, et puis encore
La manière de s'en servir
De s'en servir à deux.
Si tu voulais seulement m'approfondir ensuite un peu!

Non, non! C'est sucer la chair d'un cœur élu,
Adorer d'incurables organes
S'entrevoir avant que les tissus se fanent
En monomanes, en reclus!

Et ce n'est pas sa chair qui me serait tout.
Et je ne serais pas qu'un grand cœur pour elle,
Mais quoi s'en aller faire les fous
Dans des histoires fraternelles!

L'âme et la chair, la chair et l'âme,
C'est l'esprit édénique et fier
D'être un peu l'Homme avec la Femme.

En attendant, oh! garde-toi des coups de tête,
Oh! file ton rouet et prie et reste honnête.

Her little body knows
She's from a planet better than mine.

Oh little sister, my body's sick in its beautiful soul…

And now your piano playing, so natal,
Sets me off again!
Your ignorant, anonymous heart
Stumbles through its etudes and pop tunes
Hurting you!
Valkyries, hurry!
Valkyries of genocide and hypochondria!

Your body's a jewel, your soul's a diva,
And I'd gladly wring your neck to prove
It's true and teach you to use
Such a body and such a soul
With a man.
Afterwards, maybe, you'd like to get to know me!

No! Love gnaws at the heart,
It worships incurable organs,
It withers into a gauze of gaze,
And the dying lovers go crazy!

Her body's not the world to me, and I'm
Not the Man of her Dreams.
Why go on like idiots
Playing at sister-brother love!

Soul and body, body and soul,
Proud spirit of Eden,
Woman with Man.

In the meantime, stay straight,
Stick to your knitting, and pray.

—Allons, dernier des poètes,
Toujours enfermé tu te rendras malade!
Vois, il fait beau temps, tout le monde est dehors,
Va donc acheter deux sous d'ellébore,
Ça te fera une petite promenade.

And as for you, last of the poets,
Get out a little. You look terrible.
It's a nice enough day. People are out and about.
Take a walk to the drugstore.
Fix yourself up.

IV. Dimanches

C'est l'automne, l'automne, l'automne,
Le grand vent et toute sa séquelle
De représailles! et de musiques!…
Rideaux tirés, clôture annuelle,
Chute des feuilles, des Antigones, des Philomèles:
Mon fossoyeur, *Alas poor Yorick!*
Les remue à la pelle!…

Vivent l'Amour et les feux de paille!…

Les Jeunes Filles inviolables et frêles
Descendent vers la petite chapelle
Dont les chimériques cloches
Du joli, joli dimanche
Hygiéniquement et élégamment les appellent.

Comme tout se fait propre autour d'elles!
Comme tout en est dimanche!

Comme on se fait dur et boudeur à leur approche!…

Ah! moi, je demeure l'Ours Blanc!
Je suis venu par ces banquises
Plus pures que les communiantes en blanc…
Moi, je ne vais pas à l'église,
Moi, je suis le Grand Chancelier de l'Analyse,
Qu'on se le dise.

Pourtant, pourtant! Qu'est-ce que c'est que cette anémie?
Voyons, confiez vos chagrins à votre vieil ami…

Vraiment! Vraiment!
Ah! Je me tourne vers la mer, les éléments
Et tout ce qui n'a plus que les noirs grognements!

IV. Sundays

It's autumn, autumn, autumn,
Gales of music,
Debris of retribution!…
Curtains drawn, annual shutdowns,
Showers of leaves, of Antigones, of Philomels:
My personal grave-digger, *Alas poor Yorick!*
Rakes them into heaps…

Hurray for love and for the sweet smell of bonfires!

This pretty, pretty Sunday
Frail inviolable virgins
Stroll to the little chapel
Whose insane bells
Hygienically and elegantly draw them in.

Cleanness everywhere they go!
Sunday anywhere you look!

The closer they get, the crueler I become!…

Me, I'm still a polar bear!
I came here over ice-fields
More purely white than any little girl at her first communion…
I never go to church.
I'm warning you,
I'm the Imperial Chancellor of Empiricism.

And yet, and yet, what's up with this anemia?
Old friend, what's going on?…

I mean it! Really!
I turn to the sea, to the elements,
To the blackening growl of nothingness!

Oh! que c'est sacré!
Et qu'il y faut de grandes veillées!

Pauvre, pauvre, sous couleur d'attraits!…

Et nous, et nous,
Ivres, ivres, avant qu'émerveillés…
Qu'émerveillés et à genoux!…

Et voyez comme on tremble
Au premier grand soir
Que tout pousse au désespoir
D'en mourir ensemble!

O merveille qu'on n'a su que cacher!
Si pauvre et si brûlante et si martyre!
Et qu'on n'ose toucher
Qu'à l'aveugle, en divin délire!

O merveille.
Reste cachée, idéale violette,
L'Univers te veille,
Les générations de planètes te tettent.
De funérailles en relevailles!…

Oh! que c'est plus haut
Que ce Dieu et que la Pensée!
Et rien qu'avec ces chers yeux en haut,
Tout inconscients et couleur de pensée!…

Si frêle, si frêle!
Et tout le mortel foyer
Tout, tout ce foyer en elle!…

Oh, pardonnez-lui si, malgré elle,
Et cela tant lui sied,
Parfois ses prunelles clignent un peu

So very sacred!
So many vigils!

Paltry, paltry, in spite of all the colors!...

Drunkards, drunkards in the presence of wonders,
Kneeling, thunderstruck!...

See how we tremble,
The first of the long evenings
When despair sets in
And we know that we all die alone!

A marvel, and nothing to do but hide it!
Paltry, ardent, martyred!
Marvel we dare not touch
But with eyes shut, in Godly delirium!

O marvel. Stay hidden, ideal violet,
The Universe stands guard,
From death back to life
Generations of planets suckle you!...

So very much higher
Than God and Mind!
With nothing but eyes up there,
Dear, unconscious eyes, the color of thoughts!

Frail, so very frail!
The entirety of our deathly home
Entirely within her!...

Oh! forgive her if, in spite of herself,
—and it goes right through your heart—
Her eyes sometimes flicker and glisten,

Pour vous demander un peu
De vous apitoyer un peu!

O frêle, frêle et toujours prête
Pour ces messes dont on a fait un jeu,
Penche, penche ta chère tête, va,
Regarde les grappes des premiers lilas,
Il ne s'agit pas de conquêtes, avec moi,
Mais d'au-delà!

Oh! puissions-nous quitter la vie
Ensemble dès cette Grand'Messe,
Ecœurés de notre espèce
Qui bâille assouvie
Dès le parvis!…

Asking a little something from you,
Pity perhaps.

Frail, so very frail and always ready
For requiems we've long since made into games;
Lower your darling gaze, look down,
See these masses of lilacs;
No, I'm not looking for sex,
I'm looking for Heaven!

If only we could leave this world together
At the end of all requiems,
Sick of these gape-mouthed
Humans yawning
At the church door!...

V. Pétition

Amour absolu, carrefour sans fontaine;
Mais, à tous les bouts, d'étourdissantes fêtes foraines.

Jamais franches,
Ou le poing sur la hanche:
Avec toutes, l'amour s'échange
Simple et sans foi comme un bonjour.

O bouquets d'oranger cuirassés de satin,
Elle s'éteint, elle s'éteint,
La divine Rosace
A voir vos noces de sexes livrés à la grosse
Courir en valsant vers la fosse
Commune!… Pauvre race!

Pas d'absolu; des compromis;
Tout est pas plus, tout est permis.

Et cependant, ô des nuits, laissez-moi, Circés
Sombrement coiffées à la Titus,
Et les yeux en grand deuil comme des pensées!
Et passez,
Béatifiques Vénus
Etalées et découvrant vos gencives comme un régal,
Et bâillant des aisselles au soleil
Dans l'assourdissement des cigales!
Ou, droites, tenant sur fond violet le lotus
Des sacrilèges domestiques,
En faisant de l'index: *motus!*

Passez, passez, bien que les yeux vierges
Ne soient que cadrans d'émail bleu,
Marquant telle heure que l'on veut,
Sauf à garder pour eux, pour Elle,
Leur heure immortelle.

V. Petition

Unconditional love, a crossroads with no fountain;
But on every corner, deafening bazaars.

Uncandid,
Or arms akimbo:
It's the same with all women,
Love is a faithless exchange, a faceless greeting.

O bouquets of orange blossom armored in satin,
The stained-glass Virgin
Fades, she fades away
At the sight of your sex-weddings served up wholesale
And insane waltzes towards a common grave!
Pathetic species!

Nothing Absolute; always more compromise;
All-in-All's no more when all's allowed.

Yet some nights, for heaven's sake, leave me alone, you Circes
Darkly coiffed as Roman whores,
Eyes in deep mourning deeper than flowers!
Let me be,
Beatific Venuses,
Your legs spread, teeth bared like Turkish delights,
Armpits yawning at the sun
In the deafening drone of cicadas!
Or, standing upright against a purple background,
Holding the lotus of domestic sacrilege in one hand,
Hushing me with the index of the other.

Let me be, never mind blue virgin eyes
Are only sundials
Telling whatever time you want but one,
Their solitary proprietary She:
Eternity.

Sans doute au premier mot,
On va baisser ces yeux,
Et peut-être choir en syncope,
On est si vierge à fleur de robe
Peut-être même à fleur de peau,
Mais leur destinée est bien interlope, au nom de Dieu!

O historiques esclaves!
Oh! leur petite chambre!
Qu'on peut les en faire descendre
Vers d'autres étages,
Vers les plus frelatées des caves,
Vers les moins ange-gardien des ménages!

Et alors, le grand Suicide, à froid,
Et leur *Amen* d'une voix sans Elle,
Tout en vaquant aux petits soins secrets,
Et puis leur éternel air distrait
Leur grand air de dire: «De quoi?
«Ah! de quoi, au fond, s'il vous plaît?»

Mon Dieu, que l'Idéal
La dépouillât de ce rôle d'ange!
Qu'elle adoptât l'homme comme égal
Oh! que ses yeux ne parlent plus d'Idéal
Mais simplement d'humains échanges!
En frères et sœurs par le cœur,
Et fiancés par le passé,
Et puis unis par l'Infini!
Oh! simplement d'infinis échanges
A la fin de journées
A quatre bras moissonnées,
Quand les tambours, quand les trompettes,
Ils s'en vont sonnant la retraite,
Et qu'on prend le frais sur le pas des portes,
En vidant les pots de grès
A la santé des années mortes

Say anything you like,
They'll lower their eyes,
Even swoon sometimes,
They're virgins after all,
Down to the ground, down to the bone,
But Christ, their only future is a fall.

O epochal slaves!
Oh! their tiny bedrooms!
You could force them downstairs,
Storey by storey, all the way down
To the filthiest cellars,
To the grossest of the household gods.

In cold blood then, the big Suicide,
Everyone saying *Amen* except Her,
Everyone obsessed with little secrets,
Eternal fake bewilderments—
"What? What are you saying?
What on earth do you mean?"

My God, if only the Ideal
Would strip her of her angel wings!
If only she'd accept man as her equal…
Oh! forbid her eyes to speak of the Ideal,
Let them speak plainly of human things!
Like brothers and sisters via the heart,
And fiancés via the long-ago,
And then all of them intertwined via infinity!
Oh! infinitely simple interchanges
At the end of days
In harvesting arms
Drums and trumpets
Sounding retreat,
As we sit in the cool of the evening on doorsteps,
Raising glasses to the very good health
Of times out of mind

Qui n'ont pas laissé de regrets,
Au su de tout le canton
Que depuis toujours nous habitons,
Ton ton, ton taine, ton ton.

And no regrets,
The whole neighborhood,
And we've all lived here forever,
Tantivy, tantivy, tan-ti-vy!

VI. Simple agonie

O paria!—Et revoici les sympathies de mai.
Mais tu ne peux que te répéter, ô honte!
Et tu te gonfles et ne crèves jamais.
Et tu sais fort bien, ô paria,
Que ce n'est pas du tout ça.

Oh! que
Devinant l'instant le plus seul de la nature,
Ma mélodie, toute et unique, monte,
Dans le soir et redouble, et fasse tout ce qu'elle peut
Et dise la chose qu'est la chose,
Et retombe, et reprenne,
Et fasse de la peine,
O solo de sanglots,
Et reprenne et retombe
Selon la tâche qui lui incombe.
Oh! que ma musique
Se crucifie,
Selon sa photographie
Accoudée et mélancolique!….

Il faut trouver d'autres thèmes,
Plus mortels et plus suprêmes.
Oh! bien, avec le monde tel quel,
Je vais me faire un monde plus mortel!

Les âmes y seront à musique,
Et tous les intérêts puérilement charnels,
O fanfares dans les soirs,
Ce sera barbare,
Ce sera sans espoir.

Enquêtes, enquêtes,
Seront l'unique fête!
Qui m'en défie?

VI. Simple Agony

Pariah!—the tender feelings of May return.
But shame on you! You only repeat yourself.
You puff yourself up but never burst.
Pariah, you know damn well
Nothing matters at all.

Okay!
I have the unique music to imagine
The loneliest moment in all the world,
And the music rises into the night sky, swells
To say a thing that is, is.
And then it dies away. And then it begins again,
Breaks hearts,
O sobbing aria,
It begins again and dies away,
As it must.
God help
My crucified music
Nailed to a photograph
Of a woman staring at the moon.

Find other themes,
More deadly, more supreme.
The world is the World, okay;
I'll make a poisonous world of my own.

Musical souls,
Pedophile minds...
Cacophony,
Barbarity,
Despair.

Every holiday
An inquest and autopsy!
Why not?

J'entasse sur mon lit, les journaux, linge sale,
Dessins de mode, photographies quelconques,
Toute la capitale,
Matrice sociale.
Que nul n'intercède,
Ce ne sera jamais assez,
Il n'y a qu'un remède,
C'est de tout casser.

O fanfares dans les soirs!
Ce sera barbare,
Ce sera sans espoir.
Et nous aurons beau la piétiner à l'envi.
Nous ne serons jamais plus cruels que la vie,
Qui fait qu'il est des animaux injustement rossés,
Et des femmes à jamais laides….
Que nul n'intercède,
Il faut tout casser.

Alléluia, Terre paria.
Ce sera sans espoir,
De l'aurore au soir,
Quand il n'y en aura plus il y en aura encore,
Du soir à l'aurore.
Alléluia, Terre paria!
Les hommes de l'art
Ont dit: «Vrai, c'est trop tard.»
Pas de raison,
Pour ne pas activer sa crevaison.

Aux armes, citoyens! Il n'y a plus de RAISON:

Il prit froid l'autre automne,
S'étant attardé vers les peines des cors,
Sur la fin d'un beau jour.
Oh! ce fut pour vos cors, et ce fut pour l'automne,
Qu'il nous montra qu'«on meurt d'amour»!

I fill my bed with newspapers and dirty underwear,
Postcards and lingerie catalogues,
The whole economy,
The motherland.
Stay away;
There's no cure for me.
Only one thing left to do:
Smash everything.

Cacophony,
Barbarity,
Despair!
It's useless to rage and resist.
We could never be as cruel as life is:
Gentle animals are beaten without mercy,
And women are ugly...
Stay away from me;
It's time to smash everything.

Alleluia, Pariah Earth.
From dawn until dusk,
Nothing but despair.
First there's nothing, and then more nothing,
Dusk until dawn.
Alleluia, Pariah Earth.
The artists have declared:
"Too late."
And why not say
Doomsday.

Aux armes, citoyens! We're all INSANE.

He caught cold in the autumn,
Stayed out too late for love of the sorrowing horns
At the end of a fine day.
It was because of the hunting horns, because of the autumn,
He showed us how to die for love!

On ne le verra plus aux fêtes nationales,
S'enfermer dans l'Histoire et tirer les verrous,
Il vint trop tôt, il est reparti sans scandale;
O vous qui m'écoutez, rentrez chacun chez vous.

Holidays may come and go, but we won't see him
Locked behind the iron door of History.
He came too soon, he left with his innocence intact.
If you can read this, go home.

VII. Solo de lune

Je fume, étalé face au ciel,
Sur l'impériale de la diligence,
Ma carcasse est cahotée, mon âme danse
Comme un Ariel;
Sans miel, sans fiel, ma belle âme danse,
O routes, coteaux, ô fumées, ô vallons,
Ma belle âme, ah! récapitulons.

Nous nous aimions comme deux fous,
On s'est quitté sans en parler,
Un spleen me tenait exilé,
Et ce spleen me venait de tout. Bon.

Ses yeux disaient: «Comprenez-vous?
«Pourquoi ne comprenez-vous pas?»
Mais nul n'a voulu faire le premier pas,
Voulant trop tomber *ensemble* à genoux.
(Comprenez-vous?)

Où est-elle à cette heure?
Peut-être qu'elle pleure....
Où est-elle à cette heure?
Oh! du moins, soigne-toi, je t'en conjure!

O fraîcheur des bois le long de la route,
O châle de mélancolie, toute âme est un peu aux écoutes,
Que ma vie
Fait envie!
Cette impériale de diligence tient de la magie.

Accumulons l'irréparable!
Renchérissons sur notre sort!
Les étoiles sont plus nombreuses que le sable
Des mers où d'autres ont vu se baigner son corps;

VII. Honeymoon Solo

I'm sprawled atop a stagecoach, smoking,
Grinning at the sky;
My carcass is bouncing, my soul is dancing
Like an Ariel;
Without honey, without venom, my beautiful soul is dancing,
O highways, hilltops, smokestacks, valleys,
Beautiful soul, let's tell the tale again.

We loved each other like mooncalves,
We parted without a word;
Desolation banished me,
And desolation was everything. Good.

Her eyes said, "Do you understand?
Why don't you understand?"
But neither of us could make a move,
Wanting so badly to fall to our knees together.
(Understand?)

Where is she now?
Maybe she's crying…
Where is she now?
Baby, take care!

O coolness of the woods along the road,
O shawl of melancholy, every soul's a busybody
Green
With envy!
The top of this stagecoach really is magical.

Heap the irreparable!
Outbid the inevitable!
The stars in the sky outnumber the grains of sand
On beaches where men have seen her naked.

Tout n'en va pas moins à la Mort.
Y a pas de port.

Des ans vont passer là-dessus,
On s'endurcira chacun pour soi,
Et bien souvent et déjà je m'y vois,
On se dira: «Si j'avais su…»
Mais mariés de même, ne se fût-on pas dit:
«Si j'avais su, si j'avais su!…»?
Ah! rendez-vous maudit!
Ah! mon cœur sans issue!…
Je me suis mal conduit.

Maniaques de bonheur,
Donc, que ferons-nous? Moi de mon âme,
Elle de sa faillible jeunesse?
O vieillissante pécheresse,
Oh! que de soirs je vais me rendre infâme
En ton honneur!

Ses yeux clignaient: «Comprenez-vous?
«Pourquoi ne comprenez-vous pas?»
Mais nul n'a fait le premier pas
Pour tomber ensemble à genoux. Ah!…

La lune se lève,
O route en grand rêve!…

On a dépassé les filatures, les scieries,
Plus que les bornes kilométriques,
De petits nuages d'un rose de confiserie,
Cependant qu'un fin croissant de lune se lève,
O route de rêve, ô nulle musique…
Dans ces bois de pins où depuis
Le commencement du monde
Il fait toujours nuit,
Que de chambres propres et profondes!
Oh! pour un soir d'enlèvement!

Everything's shot to hell.
We're helpless.

Years go by,
We're both alone,
We're thick-skinned,
We say, "If only I had known…"
But suppose we *had* married, wouldn't we have said,
"If only I'd known!…"
Doomed hotel rooms!
Hapless hearts!…
I was an idiot.

Crazy for happiness,
What now? Me with my soul,
Her with her defunct virginity?
We're fucked, my dear.
The question is, how long
Do *we* loathe *me*?

Her eyes' telegraphy: "Do you understand?
Why don't you understand?"
But neither of us could move,
We never fell to our knees together. Ah!…

The moon's rising,
O highway of dreams!…

We've passed the cotton mills and the sawmills,
There's nothing left but milestones now,
Little pink candy clouds
Where the crescent moon rises,
Highway of dreams, O song of the void…
From the beginning of the world,
Eternal night
Has darkened these pinewoods,
Such tidy, such deeply hidden hotels!
O for a honeymoon!

Et je les peuple et je m'y vois,
Et c'est un beau couple d'amants,
Qui gesticulent hors la loi.

Et je passe et les abandonne,
Et me recouche face au ciel,
La route tourne, je suis Ariel,
Nul ne m'attend, je ne vais chez personne.
Je n'ai que l'amitié des chambres d'hôtel.

La lune se lève,
O route en grand rêve.
O route sans terme,
Voici le relais,
Où l'on allume les lanternes,
Où l'on boit un verre de lait,
Et fouette postillon,
Dans le chant des grillons,
Sous les étoiles de juillet.

O clair de Lune,
Noce de feux de Bengale noyant mon infortune,
Les ombres des peupliers sur la route…
Le gave qui s'écoute…
Qui s'écoute chanter…
Dans ces inondations du fleuve du Léthé…

O Solo de lune,
Vous défiez ma plume,
Oh! cette nuit sur la route;
O Étoiles, vous êtes à faire peur,
Vous y êtes toutes! toutes!
O fugacité de cette heure…
Oh! qu'il y eût moyen
De m'en garder l'âme pour l'automne qui vient!…

Voici qu'il fait très, très frais,
Oh! si à la même heure,

I fill the rooms with people, I can see us there,
A fine pair of lovers,
Gesturing obscenely.

I keep going, I leave them behind,
I lie back down again, grinning at the sky.
At a bend in the road, I'm Ariel
Going nowhere, nobody waiting for me.
My only friends are empty hotels.

The moon's rising,
O highway of dreams,
Endless highway,
Here's rest,
A little place all lit up,
A glass of milk,
And we're off again,
Into the noise of crickets
Under summer stars.

O moonlight,
Firework wedding inundating ill-luck,
Shadows of poplars along the road...
Mountain torrent listens to itself...
Hears itself singing...
Lethe...

Honeymoon solo,
Piss on my pen,
Oh! that night on the road;
O stars, you're scaring me,
You're everywhere, every one of you!
Fugacity of the hour...
I'm saving my soul if only
A soul *can* be saved until the autumn comes!...

It's getting chilly.
What if, this very minute,

Elle va de même le long des forêts,
Noyer son infortune
Dans les noces du clair de lune!...
(Elle aime tant errer tard!)
Elle aura oublié son foulard,
Elle va prendre mal, vu la beauté de l'heure!
Oh! soigne-toi, je t'en conjure!
Oh! je ne veux plus entendre cette toux!

Ah! que ne suis-je tombé à tes genoux!
Ah! que n'as-tu défailli à mes genoux!
J'eusse été le modèle des époux!
Comme le frou-frou de ta robe est le modèle des frou-frou.

She's out there, somewhere in the woods,
Drowning her sorrows in moonlight,
Marrying shadows!
(She's always liked to walk around at night!)
She'll have forgotten her scarf,
She'll catch her death, and for what? For scenery?
Honey, take care of yourself, I'm begging you!
I really can't stand that coughing anymore!

If only I had fallen at your knees!
If only you had fainted at mine!
I would have been the ultimate husband,
Just as the frou-frou of your frou-frou is the ultimate skirt.

VIII. Légende

Armorial d'anémie!
Psautier d'automne!
Offertoire de tout mon ciboire de bonheur et de génie
A cette hostie si féminine,
Et si petite toux sèche maligne,
Qu'on voit aux jours déserts, en inconnue,
Sertie en de cendreuses toilettes qui sentent déjà l'hiver,
Se fuir le long des cris surhumains de la Mer.

Grandes amours, oh! qu'est-ce encor?...

En tout cas, des lèvres sans façon,
Des lèvres déflorées,
Et quoique mortes aux chansons,
Apres encore à la curée.
Mais les yeux d'une âme qui s'est bel et bien cloîtrée.

Enfin, voici qu'elle m'honore de ses confidences.
J'en souffre plus qu'elle ne pense.

—«Mais, chère perdue, comment votre esprit éclairé
«Et le stylet d'acier de vos yeux infaillibles,
«N'ont-ils pas su percer à jour la mise en frais
«De cet économique et passager bellâtre?»

—«Il vint le premier; j'étais seule près de l'âtre;
«Son cheval attaché à la grille
«Hennissait en désespéré...»

—«C'est touchant (pauvre fille)
«Et puis après?
«Oh! regardez, là-bas, cet épilogue sous couleur de couchant;
«Et puis, vrai,
«Remarquez que dès l'automne, l'automne!

60

VIII. Legend

Anemic heraldry!
Autumn psaltery!
Offertory of my entire communion cup of joy and genius
To this feminine wafer
With her tubercular little cough…
You can see her on bleak days, her incognito,
Her cindery outfit stinking of ice,
Rushing past the superhuman screech of the Sea.

Endless love…so what?

Anyway, a pretty mouth,
Debauched lips…
She can't sing,
But she can suck.
And still her eyes remain the perfect flowers of a beautiful cloister.

Finally, she confides in me.
It's killing me.

"Beloved fallen angel, how could your sharp mind
And the stiletto of your eyes
Have failed to see right through
Such a cheapskate fancy-pants?"

"He was my first; I was alone by the fireplace;
His poor horse was tied to our fence,
Neighing in despair…"

"Very touching (poor girl),
And what happened next?
Hey, look over there, an epilogue pretending to be a sunset!
No getting around it,
When autumn comes, it's really autumn.

«Les casinos,
«Qu'on abandonne
«Remisent leur piano;
«Hier l'orchestre attaqua
«Sa dernière polka,
«Hier, la dernière fanfare
«Sanglotait vers les gares…»

(Oh! comme elle est maigrie!
Que va-t-elle devenir?
Durcissez, durcissez,
Vous, caillots de souvenir!)

—«Allons, les poteaux télégraphiques
«Dans les grisailles de l'exil
«Vous serviront de pleureuses de funérailles;
«Moi, c'est la saison qui veut que je m'en aille,
«Voici l'hiver qui vient.
«Ainsi soit-il.
«Ah! soignez-vous! Portez-vous bien.

«Assez! assez!
«C'est toi qui as commencé!

«Tais-toi! Vos moindres clins d'yeux sont des parjures.
«Laisse! Avec vous autres rien ne dure.
«Va, je te l'assure,
«Si je t'aimais, ce serait par gageure.

«Tais-toi! tais-toi!
«On n'aime qu'une fois!»

Ah! voici que l'on compte enfin avec Moi!

Ah! ce n'est plus l'automne, alors,
Ce n'est plus l'exil.
C'est la douceur des légendes, de l'âge d'or,

Abandoned
Casinos
Pack away their pianos;
Yesterday the orchestra mangled
One last polka,
Yesterday the last diminuendo
Sobbed into the trains."

(How terribly thin she is!
What's to become of her?
Blood-clots of memory, I command you,
Grow harder and harder still!)

"Come away, in the gray light of exile
Telegraph poles will march
In your funeral procession;
As for me, it's time I was going,
Winter's coming.
So it goes.
Look after yourself, baby. Stay warm

"Enough! enough!
You were the one who started it, after all!

"Shut up! Even your eyelids are perjuries.
Let it go. Nothing lasts for people like you.
Look, I'm telling you,
If ever I loved you, it was all a joke.

"Shut up! Shut up!
In a whole lifetime, you only love once!"

And now at last she really has to deal with Me!

Oh, I see…it isn't autumn anymore,
It isn't exile.
It's the sweetness of legends, of the Golden Age,

Des légendes des Antigones,
Douceur qui fait qu'on se demande:
«Quand donc cela se passait-il?»

C'est des légendes, c'est des gammes perlées,
Qu'on m'a tout enfant enseignées,
Oh! rien, vous dis-je, des estampes,
Les bêtes de la terre et les oiseaux du ciel
Enguirlandant les majuscules d'un Missel,
Il n'y a pas là tant de quoi saigner?

Saigner? moi pétri du plus pur limon de Cybèle!
Moi qui lui eusse été dans tout l'art des Adams
Des Édens aussi hyperboliquement fidèle
Que l'est le Soleil chaque soir envers l'Occident!…

Of Antigones,
A sweetness that makes you wonder:
"When did all this actually happen?"

It's legends, pearly scales
I learned as a child,
It's nothing, I'm telling you, it's pictures,
Beasts of the earth and birds of the air
Woven into the letters of a prayer-book,
Enough to make you bleed?

Bleed? I was molded out of Cybele's purest clay!
Me? I was Adam's masterpiece in Eden,
I was faithful to her in absolute hyperbole,
As the setting sun is faithful to the West!...

IX.

Oh! qu'une, d'Elle-même, un beau soir, sût venir
Ne voyant plus que boire à mes lèvres, ou mourir!...

Oh! Baptême!
Oh! baptême de ma Raison d'être!
Faire naître un «Je t'aime!»
Et qu'il vienne à travers les hommes et les dieux,
Sous ma fenêtre,
Baissant les yeux!

Qu'il vienne, comme à l'aimant la foudre,
Et dans mon ciel d'orage qui craque et qui s'ouvre,
Et alors, les averses lustrales jusqu'au matin,
Le grand clapissement des averses toute la nuit! Enfin

Qu'Elle vienne! et, baissant les yeux
Et s'essuyant les pieds
Au seuil de notre église, ô mes aïeux
Ministres de la Pitié,
Elle dise:

«Pour moi, tu n'es pas comme les autres hommes,
«Ils sont ces messieurs, toi tu viens des cieux.
«Ta bouche me fait baisser les yeux
«Et ton port me transporte
«Et je m'en découvre des trésors!
«Et je sais parfaitement que ma destinée se borne
«(Oh, j'y suis déjà bien habituée!)
«A te suivre jusqu'à ce que tu te retournes,
«Et alors t'exprimer comment tu es!

«Vraiment je ne songe pas au reste; j'attendrai
«Dans l'attendrissement de ma vie faite exprès.

IX. The Loves

If only of her own free will one evening
She'd come to drink at my lips or die!...

Oh! Baptism!
Baptism of my will to live!
Give birth to even one "I love you!"
Let it find its way through men and gods
All the way to my window
And lower its eyes.

May it come like lightning to a magnet
Out of storm clouds and a broken sky,
Lustral downpours until morning,
Thunderclaps all night long! At last

Let her come! And lowering her eyes
And wiping her feet
At the threshold of our church, O my ancestors,
Ministers of pity,
Let her say:

"You're not like the others, they,
They're 'gentlemen,' but you're an angel.
Your kisses make me faint,
And the way you carry yourself,
So beautiful, it goes right through me!
I know it all too well, I'm doomed
(And I don't mind)
To follow you until one day you turn around
And I explain you to yourself!

"I never think of anything else; I just keep waiting
Here in this inexpressible tenderness.

«Que je te dise seulement que depuis des nuits je pleure,
«Et que mes sœurs ont bien peur que je n'en meure.

«Je pleure dans les coins, je n'ai plus goût à rien;
«Oh, j'ai tant pleuré dimanche dans mon paroissien!

«Tu me demandes pourquoi toi et non un autre,
«Ah! laisse, c'est bien toi et non un autre.

«J'en suis sûre comme du vide insensé de mon cœur
«Et comme de votre air mortellement moqueur.»

Ainsi, elle viendrait, évadée, demi-morte,
Se rouler sur le paillasson que j'ai mis à cet effet devant ma porte.
Ainsi, elle viendrait à Moi avec des yeux absolument fous,
Et elle me suivrait avec ces yeux-là partout, partout!

"I'm telling you I cry all night every night,
And my sisters are scared I'll die.

"I cry in the corners, I starve myself,
Last Sunday at church I soaked my prayer-book with tears!

"And now you ask me why *you* and not somebody else.
Christ! There *is* nobody else.

"I'm as sure of it as I'm sure of the dead place in my heart,
The void that is you."

So she'd come to me, fugitive, half-dead,
Convulsed on the doormat.
So she'd come to me, wild-eyed
And, wild-eyed, follow me everywhere, everywhere.

X

O géraniums diaphanes, guerroyeurs sortilèges,
Sacrilèges monomanes!
Emballages, dévergondages, douches! O pressoirs
Des vendanges des grands soirs!
Layettes aux abois,
Thyrses au fond des bois!
Transfusions, représailles,
Relevailles, compresses et l'éternelle potion,
Angelus! n'en pouvoir plus
De débâcles nuptiales! de débâcles nuptiales!…

Et puis, ô mes amours,
A moi, son tous les jours,
O ma petite mienne, ô ma quotidienne,
Dans mon petit intérieur,
C'est-à-dire plus jamais ailleurs!
O ma petite quotidienne!…

Et quoi encore? Oh du génie!
Improvisations aux insomnies!

Et puis? L'observer dans le monde,
Et songer dans les coins:
«Oh! qu'elle est loin! Oh! qu'elle est belle!
«Oh! qui est-elle? A qui est-elle?
«Oh! quelle inconnue! Oh! lui parler! Oh! l'emmener!»
(Et, en effet, à la fin du bal,
Elle me suivrait d'un air tout simplement fatal.)

Et puis, l'éviter des semaines
Après lui avoir fait de la peine,
Et lui donner des rendez-vous
Et nous refaire un chez nous.

X. The Loves

Diaphanous geranium, magical warfare,
Maniacal sacrilege!
Sprints to the finish line, debaucheries, douches! O wine-press
Of the finest evening of my life!
Layettes at bay,
Dildos wrapped in sacred laurel leaves!
Transfusions, reprisals,
Purifications, bandages and holy oil,
Angelus! The end of them all,
Marriage debacles, marriage debacles!…

And then, oh my love,
Every single day, my love,
My little, my each and every,
My deep inside and nowhere else,
My every single day!…

Anything else? Oh genius!
Improvisational insomnias!

And then what? Watching her out in the world,
I daydreamed in the shadows:
"How unapproachable she is! How beautiful!
Who is she? To whom does she belong?
What a beautiful stranger! Speak to her, Jules, carry her away!"
(As it turned out, when the dance was over
She followed me without a word. She simply followed me.)

And then I couldn't get rid of her.
For weeks I avoided her. She was so hurt,
I agreed to meet with her,
I agreed to live with her.

Et puis, la perdre des mois et des mois,
A ne plus reconnaître sa voix!…

Oui, le Temps salit tout,
Mais, hélas! sans en venir à bout.

Hélas! hélas! et plus la faculté d'errer,
Hypocondrie et pluie,
Et seul sous les vieux cieux,
De me faire le fou,
Le fou sans feux ni lieux
(Le pauvre, pauvre fou sans amours!)
Pour, alors, tomber bien bas
A me purifier la chair,
Et exulter au petit jour
En me fuyant en chemin de fer,
O Belles-Lettres, ô Beaux-Arts,
Ainsi qu'un Ange à part!

J'aurai passé ma vie le long des quais
A faillir m'embarquer
Dans de bien funestes histoires,
Tout cela pour l'amour
De mon cœur fou de la gloire d'amour.

Oh! qu'ils sont pittoresques les trains manqués!…

Oh! qu'ils sont «A bientôt! à bientôt!»
Les bateaux
Du bout de la jetée!…

De la jetée charpentée
Contre la mer,
Comme ma chair
Contre l'amour.

And then *she* was gone for months.
When she came home, I couldn't even recognize her voice!

Time shits on everything,
And then it keeps on shitting.

Alas, alas! And no legs,
Only hypochondria and rain,
All alone beneath a senile sky,
Makes a fool of me,
A fool without a home
(Poor fool, poor loveless fool!)
And then I fall on my face
To purify my flesh,
To rejoice at dawn,
To escape myself on a train,
O poetry, O Beaux-Arts,
An angel set apart!

I shall have spent my life in railway stations
Nearly departing
For catastrophes,
All for love
And my heart haloed with the madness of love.

Nothing is quite so beautiful as the trains I've missed!...

"So long!"
The boats
At the end of the pier!...

The pier
Hates the ocean,
My skin
Hates love.

XI. Sur une défunte

Vous ne m'aimeriez pas, voyons,
Vous ne m'aimeriez pas plus,
Pas plus, entre nous,
Qu'une fraternelle Occasion?…

—Ah! elle ne m'aime pas!
Ah! elle ne ferait pas le premier pas
Pour que nous tombions ensemble à genoux.

Si elle avait rencontré seulement
A, B, C ou D, au lieu de Moi,
Elle les eût aimés uniquement!

Je les vois, je les vois…

Attendez! Je la vois,
Avec les nobles A, B, C ou D.
Elle était née pour chacun d'eux.
C'est lui, Lui, quel qu'il soit,
Elle le reflète;
D'un air parfait, elle secoue la tête
Et dit que rien, rien ne peut lui déraciner
Cette étonnante destinée.

C'est Lui; elle lui dit:
«Oh! tes yeux, ta démarche!
«Oh! le son fatal de ta voix!
«Voilà si longtemps que je te cherche!
«Oh! c'est bien Toi! cette fois!…»

Il baisse un peu sa bonne lampe,
Il la ploie, Elle, vers son cœur,
Il la baise à la tempe
Et à la place de son orphelin cœur.

XI. Dead Woman

Be honest now, just between you and me,
You wouldn't love me,
You'd *never* love me as anything
More than a brother?…

She doesn't love me!
She'd never once consider the possibility
Of us falling to our knees together.

If only she'd met
A, B, C, or D instead of Me,
She'd have loved them passionately!

I see them, I see them…

Wait! I see her
With the lordlings A, B, C, and D.
She was made for each of them.
It is he, He, whichever one he is,
She basks in him;
She is perfected, she tilts her head,
She says that nothing in the world
Could separate them. It's amazing. It's destiny.

It's He; she says to him:
"Oh! Your eyes, your stride!
Oh! the fine fatedness in your voice!
You'll never know how long I've searched for you!
Oh Thou, beloved, this time it's really you!…"

He turns down the light of his lamp a little,
He rests her head on his breast,
He kisses her brow, he kisses
Her orphan heart.

Il l'endort avec des caresses tristes,
Il l'apitoie avec de petites plaintes,
Il a des considérations fatalistes,
Il prend à témoin tout ce qui existe,
Et puis voici que l'heure tinte.

Pendant que je suis dehors
A errer avec elle au cœur,
A m'étonner peut-être
De l'obscurité de sa fenêtre.

Elle est chez lui, et s'y sent chez elle.
Et, comme on vient de le voir,
Elle l'aime, éperdument fidèle,
Dans toute sa beauté des soirs!…

Je les ai vus! Oh! ce fut trop complet!
Elle avait l'air trop trop fidèle
Avec ses grands yeux tout en reflets
Dans sa figure toute nouvelle!

Et je ne serais qu'un pis-aller,

Et je ne serais qu'un pis-aller,
Comme l'est mon jour dans le Temps,
Comme l'est ma place dans l'Espace;
Et l'on ne voudrait pas que j'accommodasse
De ce sort vraiment dégoûtant!…

Non, non! pour Elle, tout ou rien!
Et je m'en irai donc comme un fou,
A travers l'automne qui vient,
Dans le grand vent où il y a tout!

Je me dirai: Oh! à cette heure,
Elle est bien loin, elle pleure,
Le grand vent se lamente aussi,

He lulls her to sleep with sad caresses,
He breaks her heart with little moans,
He's a nihilist,
He questions the existence of everything.
And then the clock strikes.

Meanwhile, I'm in the street,
Walking aimlessly, thinking of her,
And maybe I'm surprised
To find her windows dark.

She's at his place, making herself at home.
You can see for yourself
She's madly in love, in all
Her evening beauty, with *him*!…

I saw them! I couldn't stand it!
She looked besotted,
Making big eyes
With a brand new face!

And I would never be anything to her but a last resort,

I would only be her last resort,
My days on earth a pissing-place,
Time and Space themselves a pissing-place,
I couldn't stand it,
And neither could you!…

No, when it comes to Her,
It's all or nothing. I'm walking away
Like a crazy man through the coming autumn
Into fierce gales of everything!

I'll tell myself: At this very moment,
She's far away, she's weeping,
The gale-force winds are weeping too,

Et moi je suis seul dans ma demeure,
Avec mon noble cœur tout transi,
Et sans amour et sans personne,
Car tout est misère, tout est automne,
Tout est endurci et sans merci.

Et, si je t'avais aimée ainsi,
Tu l'aurais trouvée trop bien bonne! Merci!

And I'm alone with my noble heart
In a cold room
And no love, nobody here at all,
Everything's misery, everything's autumn,
Everything's merciless.

If I'd loved you exactly this way
It would've been too much. Thanks anyway!

XII.

Get thee to a nunnery: why wouldst thou be a
breeder of sinners? I am myself indifferent
honest; but yet I could accuse me of such
things, that it were better my mother had not
borne me. […] We are arrant knaves, all; believe
none of us. Go thy ways to a nunnery.

HAMLET

Noire bise, averse glapissante,
Et fleuve noir, et maisons closes,
Et quartiers sinistres comme des Morgues,
Et l'Attardé qui à la remorque traîne
Toute la misère du cœur et des choses,
Et la souillure des innocentes qui traînent,
Et crie à l'averse: «Oh! arrose, arrose
«Mon cœur si brûlant, ma chair si intéressante!»

Oh, elle, mon cœur et ma chair, que fait-elle?…

Oh! si elle est dehors par ce vilain temps,
De quelles histoires trop humaines rentre-t-elle?
Et si elle est dedans,
A ne pas pouvoir dormir par ce grand vent,
Pense-t-elle au Bonheur,
Au bonheur à tout prix
Disant: tout plutôt que mon cœur reste ainsi incompris?

Soigne-toi, soigne-toi! pauvre cœur aux abois.

(Langueurs, débilité, palpitations, larmes,
Oh! cette misère de vouloir être notre femme!)

O pays, ô famille!
Et l'âme toute tournée

XII.

Get thee to a nunnery: why wouldst thou be a
breeder of sinners? I am myself indifferent
honest; but yet I could accuse me of such
things, that it were better my mother had not
borne me. [...] We are arrant knaves, all: believe
none of us. Go thy ways to a nunnery.

HAMLET

Pitch-black northern gale and howling downpour,
Pitch-black river, abandoned houses,
Neighborhoods as sinister as Morgues,
And the Latecomer lugging all
The misery of his heart, of reality itself,
Of the rape of hapless girls,
He shouts into the downpour, "Drown
My burning heart, dowse my so very interesting skin!"

And what about her, my real heart, my actual skin, what is *she* doing?...

If she's outdoors in this filthy weather,
From what human, all-too-human filth is she returning?
And if she's indoors,
Tossing and turning in her bed, frightened by the wind,
Is she thinking of Happiness,
Happiness at any cost,
Saying: "I could stand anything, if only one time someone knew my heart?"

Poor cornered animal heart, look out!

(Languors, debility, palpitations, tears,
Miserable haphazard will to be our wife!)

O nation, O family!
And the overthrown soul

D'héroïques destinées
Au delà des saintes vieilles filles,
Et pour cette année!

Nuit noire, maisons closes, grand vent,
Oh! dans un couvent, dans un couvent!

Un couvent dans ma ville natale
Douce de vingt mille âmes à peine,
Entre le lycée et la préfecture
Et vis-à-vis la cathédrale,
Avec ces anonymes en robes grises,
Dans la prière, le ménage, les travaux de couture;
Et que cela suffise…
Et méprise sans envie
Tout ce qui n'est pas cette vie de Vestale
Provinciale,
Et marche à jamais glacée,
Les yeux baissés.

Oh! je ne puis voir ta petite scène fatale à vif,
Et ton pauvre air dans ce huis-clos,
Et tes tristes petits gestes instinctifs,
Et peut-être incapable de sanglots!

Oh! ce ne fut pas et ce ne peut être,
Oh! tu n'es pas comme les autres,
Crispées aux rideaux de leur fenêtre
Devant le soleil couchant qui dans son sang se vautre!
Oh! tu n'as pas l'âge,
Oh! dis, tu n'auras jamais l'âge,
Oh! tu me promets de rester sage comme une image?…

La nuit est à jamais noire,
Le vent est grandement triste,
Tout dit la vieille histoire
Qu'il faut être deux au coin du feu,
Tout bâcle un hymne fataliste,

Of fate itself, of elderly
Virgin saints overthrown,
It's over.

Pitch-black night, abandoned houses, northern gale,
To a nunnery, to a nunnery!

A nunnery in my hometown,
Which is a sweet town, very small,
Barely twenty thousand souls between
The school and city hall and the cathedral
Where anonymous, colorless women
Pray, sew, sweep;
That's all...
Hatred without envy,
Vestal virgin life
In the middle of nowhere
Walking on ice,
Eyes down.

I cannot stand to look into the glooms of your life.
The scenarios of wretchedness behind closed doors,
The pathetic gestures
And the weeping without tears.

It never was and it never will be,
You're not like the others,
Clawing at curtains
To see the sun setting in its own blood!
You're not that old,
Promise you'll never be that old,
Promise you'll always be as good as gold!...

The night is black forever now,
The wind is immensely sad,
Everything tells the old story
That we must be the couple huddled in a corner,
Everything is a botched hymn of fate,

Mais toi, il ne faut pas que tu t'abandonnes,
A ces vilains jeux!…

A ces grandes pitiés du mois de novembre!
Reste dans ta petite chambre,
Passe, à jamais glacée,
Tes beaux yeux irréconciliablement baissés.

Oh! qu'elle est là-bas, que la nuit est noire!
Que la vie est une étourdissante foire!
Que toutes sont créature, et que tout est routine!

Oh! que nous mourrons!

Eh bien, pour aimer ce qu'il y a d'histoires
Derrière ces beaux yeux d'orpheline héroïne,
O Nature, donne-moi la force et le courage
De me croire en âge,
O Nature, relève-moi le front!
Puisque, tôt ou tard, nous mourrons…

But you, *you* must never accept it,
Never sing along!...

Infinite pathos of the month of November!
Stay home, safe in your little room,
Forever frozen,
Your beautiful eyes forever looking down.

She is somewhere out there in the pitch-black night!
Life is a deafening funfair!
What animals women are, I'm bored of it.

We all die!

All right then, we must love whatever stories we find
In the beautiful orphan's eye,
O Nature, give me the courage and the strength
To be old enough,
Nature, lift me up!
Sooner or later, we all die...

Translator's Afterword

This is the saddest story I have ever heard.
—Ford Madox Ford, *The Good Soldier*

Over the months I devoted to these translations, this first sentence
of the twentieth century's most perfect novel was always in my
thoughts. Exactly why this should be the case became a guide to me,
a way to reach these final dozen poems by Jules Laforgue, a means to
understand that his ultimate accomplishment, *Derniers Vers*, is the
expression of a new form of sorrow born of an entirely new kind of
pain. Ford's novel, once described by John Rodker as "the finest French
novel in the English language," discovers an irony on the far side of
irony by taking sadness to an implacably logical extreme. The result
is a formal perfection, obviating all precedents. *Derniers Vers*, in the
heartbroken discipline of its free verse forms, discovers an eloquence on
the far, indeed on the posthumous side of eloquence, by carrying pain
to its autumnal paradise. The result? A Dada in advance of Dada.

> The artists have declared:
> "Too late."
> And why not say
> Doomsday.
>   ("Simple Agony")

The result? A Postmodernism in advance of Modernism, an aftermath
to obviate the avant-garde.

First to last, these twelve poems embody but a single moment.

> Okay!
> I have the unique music to imagine
> The loneliest moment in all the world…
>   ("Simple Agony")

Protracted to the point of exquisite anguish, enormous in its human detail, awful in its intractable substance, this moment is one of instantaneous and absolute transgressions. Everything human, everything gendered, everything natural, is immediately unrecognizable afterwards and evermore.

> Chautauquas, Mrs. Eddys, Dr. Dowies, Comstocks,
> societies for the prevention of all human activities
> are impossible in the wake of Laforgue. And he is
> therefore an exquisite poet, a deliverer of the nations,
> a Numa Pompilius, a father of light.
> —Ezra Pound, "Irony, Laforgue, and Some Satire"

Thus transgressive, the moment of *Derniers Vers* is the luminous threshold of a structural agon. The book begins, with "The Winter Ahead," in a sodden, chilly borderland between autumn and winter. A dozen poems later, the book concludes exactly there: "Infinite pathos of the month of November!" The book begins in a dismal transit from romantic pastoral to unreal city.

> How in drizzling rain, all my chimney stones!…
> I mean smokestacks…
> ("The Winter Ahead")

And the book remains in transit all the way.

> My days on earth a pissing-place,
> Time and Space themselves a pissing-place…
> ("Dead Woman")

There is no escaping the fact that a moment thus protracted, thus overfilled then flayed, must truly be in throes. The winter ahead is death itself, and *Derniers Vers* intends to keep that death at bay. These dozen poems are a desperate and darling delay. True enough—T.S. Eliot was a great admirer of Laforgue's early work, most specifically of the harlequinade of *Les Complaintes*. (One only needs to read "*Complainte des pianos…*" to find every single cadence of Prufrock already ready to hand.) But screw the New Criticism and its fear of death disguised as a tradition. Jules Laforgue, while writing *Derniers Vers*, damn well knew that he was dying and that his bride was dying too. (Laforgue was married to Leah Lee on New Year's Eve, 1886. He died of tuberculosis in August of 1887. Leah died of the very same illness ten months later.) Desperate but undespairing, Laforgue turned his gift against Time and Space themselves, meaning to fill them each to bursting with every idiom, image and attitude at his command. Poetic innovation, when it is real, is the product of unimagined pressures which, mercilessly and suddenly, force the imagination to change its tune. The free verse innovations of *Derniers Vers* are a changed tune and an unexpected, sudden mercy.

The inventions of Jules Laforgue's anguish have been wonderful blessings and wide permissions to the art of poetry, from High Modernism to the present day. (The only difficulty, *sans aucun doute*, is that Laforgue remains very far ahead of us all. We have yet, in any language, to conjure a poet capable of such reckless discipline.) The brazen pastiche of *Derniers Vers* began to embolden "The Waste Land" before Eliot was even born. And thinking of "The Waste Land," whose original title was "He Do the Police in Different Voices," I cannot help but note that it is the Laforgue of *Derniers Vers* who first adventured upon a cacophony of voices unrestrainedly. In these final dozen poems of his, one is never quite sure who is speaking, or to whom. Is it He? Is it She? Is it anyone at all? Misogyny morphs into self-loathing. Ophelia becomes Antigone and then becomes a singular orphaned eye. In the course of my translating, I slowly learned to be careless—almost as careless as Laforgue himself. Not knowing, one is free to hear. Indeterminacy becomes pleasurable on the far side of care. And over there, high diction and low diction intertwine like side-by-side roses. Learnedness finds the naked truth of kitsch, and kitsch begins to learn the tragedy of knowing anything at all.

> Goodbye vineyards, goodbye wicker baskets
> And Watteau petticoats tossed under chestnut trees.
> ("The Winter Ahead")

On the far side of care, in the shameless coupling of culture and kitsch, of eloquence and stammer, we find Postmodernism already underway and hotly welcoming. Page through these poems. Without *Derniers Vers*, how would Bill Knott have found his Naomi, the muse whose "shoulders are petty crimes"? How would John Ashbery have articulated his enigmatic He, "unforgettable as a shooting star" and "known as 'Liverlips'"? How would Barbara Guest have sent her "Knight of the Swan" into a tenement? And the be-bop phasings of Robert Creeley's *For Love*, pendent from tensile chords of perfect rhyme, how could they have come to pass without the first permission of Jules Laforgue's rigorous musical abandon?

Ezra Pound once famously avowed that "all that matters is the quality of the emotion." It is the essential and endlessly original quality of *Derniers Vers* to have, in clear-eyed and clear-minded desperation, invented a wholly new emotion: the sorrow of life as it never could be and never shall be lived.

> Nothing is quite so beautiful as the trains I've missed!
>   ("The Loves")

Detailing as it does the absolute impossibility of human happiness, *Derniers Vers* restores that happiness to its inaccessible and perfect absolute. Here is a Platonism to overthrow all philosophy, Plato included. The details are excruciating because they are undeniable, emblems of a world we have interpreted unto exhaustion, yet it is for just that reason that Laforgue, alone among poets, can be said to have *proven* that happiness is real. It simply rests safely beyond our ability to experience it. Happiness is the God we cannot know, the God who has forgotten us long since.

> God help
> My crucified music
> Nailed to a photograph
> Of a woman staring at the moon.
>   ("Simple Agony")

The music of Jules Laforgue, free beyond the drab responsibilities of freedom, attenuated not into a cry but into an irrevocable exhalation, remains just beyond our hearing, forever more than new.

About the Author

Jules Laforgue, the second of eleven children, was born on August 16, 1860, in Montevideo, Uruguay, where his father taught French. In 1866, the family moved back to France, but only for a year. His parents and younger siblings returned to Uruguay; Jules and his elder brother Emile remained behind in Tarbes, their father's hometown, in the care of cousins. At the age of sixteen, Laforgue moved to Paris. Although he failed his baccalaureate exams three times, he had become an avid reader of the French classics as well as of Shakespeare, Whitman and Schopenhauer. He began to publish poems in 1879; by 1880, he was a recognized poet. The next year, he moved to Berlin, where he had found employment as "reader" to the Empress Augusta. In 1886 Laforgue married Leah Lee, an English governess, and they settled in Paris. Laforgue died there on August 20, 1887. He had published three collections of poetry during his lifetime: *The Laments* (1885); *The Imitation of Our Lady the Moon* (1886); and *The Fairy Council* (1886). *Last Verses* was published posthumously by his friends.

François Camoin

Donald Revell is Professor of English and Director of Creative Writing programs at the University of Nevada-Las Vegas. Winner of the PEN USA Translation Award for his translation of Rimbaud's *A Season in Hell* and two-time winner of the PEN USA Award for Poetry, he has also won the Academy of American Poets Lenore Marshall Prize and is a former fellow of the Ingram Merrill and Guggenheim Foundations. Additionally, he has twice been granted fellowships in poetry from the National Endowment for the Arts. Former editor-in-chief of *Denver Quarterly*, he now serves as poetry editor of *Colorado Review*. Revell lives in the desert south of Las Vegas with his wife, poet Claudia Keelan, and their children Benjamin Brecht and Lucie Ming.

Last Verses
by Jules Laforgue
Translated by Donald Revell

Cover and interior text set in Adobe Sanvito Pro and Adobe Jenson Pro.

Book offset printed by Thomson-Shore, Inc., Dexter, Michigan
on Glatfelter Natures Natural 60# archival quality recycled paper
to the Green Press Initiative standard.

Cover Art by Odilon Redon:
Five Butterflies, 1912
Watercolor on wove paper, 270 mm x 211 mm (10.2 x 8.3 inches).

Cover and interior design by Ken Keegan.

Omnidawn Publishing
Richmond, California
2011

Ken Keegan & Rusty Morrison, Co-Publishers & Senior Editors
Cassandra Smith, Poetry Editor & Book Designer
Sara Mumolo, Poetry Editor & Poetry Features Editor
Gillian Hamel, Poetry Editor & Senior Blog Editor
Jared Alford, Facebook Editor
Peter Burghardt, Bookstore Outreach Manager
Juliana Paslay, Bookstore Outreach & Features Writer
Craig Santos Perez, Media Consultant